P9-DDG-468

COLORING
DEVOTIONAL

Draw
Near
to
God

BroadStreet
PUBLISHING

BroadStreet Publishing Group LLC
Racine, Wisconsin, USA
Broadstreetpublishing.com

Draw Near to God

© 2016 by BroadStreet Publishing

ISBN 978-1-4245-4984-9

Devotional entries composed by Shannon Lindsay and Michelle Winger.

Design by Chris Garborg | garborgdesign.com
Compiled and edited by Michelle Winger | literallyprecise.com

Printed in China.

16   17   18   19   20   21   22   7   6   5   4   3   2   1

Introduction

Life is full of demands. Appointments, deadlines, obligations, and constant digital chatter occupy every moment and build a mountain of unhealthy stress and tension. Research shows that coloring can be an effective stress reducer, but true rest and peace are found in God. This coloring devotional incorporates these two ideas in one beautiful book.

Spend time reflecting on the truth of God's Word and be filled with the joy and peace found in his presence. Express your creativity freely as you fill the intricate images with the beauty of color.

Simple Acceptance

If you confess with your mouth that Jesus
is Lord and believe in your heart that God
raised him from the dead, you will be saved.
For with the heart one believes and is
justified, and with the mouth one confesses
and is saved.

ROMANS 10:9-10 ESV

How can it be that a humble prayer, a simple and yet
astounding desire to lay down one's life and take up a life
like Jesus Christ, establishes our eternity in the kingdom of
heaven? Is it possible that such an act can really guarantee
salvation?

Our acceptance into God's family begins with this one act, yet
it can feel too simplistic, too easy. We live in a world where,
more often than not, we get what we deserve and nothing
comes easy.

Sometimes, because we can't believe that acceptance can come from such a simple act, we reconstruct the gospel. We want to feel like we deserve God's grace, or that we have earned it, or that we've traded fairly. We build another set of requirements: more praying, more giving, more reading, more serving. Quiet time. Worship team. Children's ministry. Bible study. All of these habits are good and Christ-like, but they don't guarantee *more acceptance*. Not from God, anyway.

Paul emphasized how simple the path to salvation really is in his letter to the Roman church: if you believe it, say it. There is no other way. Believe that your simple and earnest prayer assures your acceptance. It is this simple. God's Word promises that it is.

> *God, I find it difficult to believe in the simplicity of your requirement for acceptance. As I spend time coloring today, remind me of the things I am doing to try to gain your approval. Help me to understand that you accept me simply because I believe.*

Draw near
to God,
and he will
draw near
to you.

JAMES 4:8 ESV

Good Plans

For I know the plans I have for you,
declares the LORD,
plans for welfare and not for evil,
to give you a future and a hope.

Jeremiah 29:11 ESV

There are two types of people in the world: those who can pack their bags at a moment's notice and take a last-minute vacation to Paris, and those who need months of planning and organization. You may be willing to do either one—it is a trip to Paris, after all!—but under which conditions would you most enjoy yourself? Could you trust that it would be everything you would've planned for yourself if you didn't thoroughly prepare it?

What if a well-travelled Parisian had personally chosen every hotel, restaurant, and attraction based on your individual tastes? Would you relax, knowing that the trip would be exciting yet safe, surprising yet tailored, unexpected yet promising?

When we consider our future, it can be difficult to trust that things will work out the way we desire. If only we could know that the plans for our future are certain! Consider that God knows the future, he knows you, and he knows exactly what you need. Read those words carefully… he knows exactly what you *need*. You won't always get what you want, but he can give you what you *need*.

If you stick to the guidebook, your life might be just fine. You'll be a happy tourist in this world. But if you trust God, the one who knows you and your destination perfectly, you will see the secret places and hidden gems known only to the one who created them. Have faith. He has a plan that will take you places you never could have imagined. There is no better way!

God, I believe that you have the best plan in mind for my life. There are so many things I think I need, but I want you to show me what you know is best.

Child of God

All who are led by the Spirit of God are children of God. So you have not received a spirit that makes you fearful slaves. Instead, you received God's Spirit when he adopted you as his own children. Now we call him, "Abba, Father." For his Spirit joins with our spirit to affirm that we are God's children. And since we are his children, we are his heirs.

Romans 8:14-17 NLT

God is a good Father! He loves you with a love that is matchless and unwavering. Our earthly fathers have important jobs; primarily, they guide us to the love of our heavenly Father. Whether a devoted man's guidance models the Father's truly perfect and boundless love, or a flawed man's brokenness leads us to the Father's healing and compassionate love, both lead us home as children of God.

With lives submitted to Jesus Christ, we have the privilege of the Holy Spirit leading us in truth and in action. This Spirit, as Paul describes, is proof that we are adopted into God's family as children and heirs. We can take hold of our claim as God's precious and beloved children.

God teaches what true fatherhood looks like: loving authority, gentle guidance, unending grace, tender compassion, fierce protection, and perfect faithfulness.

Know that you are a child of God. Walk in the privileges of an heiress: full acceptance, spotless purity, humble confidence, eternal redemption, and an inheritance of life everlasting.

> *Father, thank you for your*
> *immeasurable greatness. You have*
> *adopted me into your family and I am so*
> *grateful to be called your child. You truly*
> *are the perfect Father.*

"Peace
I leave
with you,
my peace
I give you."

JOHN 14:27 NIV

Made to Be

The fruit of the Spirit is love, joy, peace, patience, kindness, goodness, faithfulness, gentleness, self-control; against such things there is no law.

Galatians 5:22-23 ESV

Making applesauce with autumn's abundant apple harvest is a beloved pastime across northern parts of America. Experts have developed award-winning recipes whose secret, they say, is combining multiple varieties of apples to produce a complex flavor profile. The result is a balance of the tart, sweet, crisp, mellow, and bold flavors for which apples are so well-loved. Each variety of apple is essential to the applesauce; their distinct flavors mesh into a delicious thing of beauty.

In the applesauce of God's ministry, each believer's spiritual fruit flavor-profile is essential. The fruit of the Spirit looks, tastes, feels, smells, and sounds different for each of us. In some, joy is a loud shout of excitement; in others it is quiet worship. One believer's kindness might feel soft while another's is firm. Peace can be expressed in as many ways as there are to use an apple.

When we compare the evidence of our fruit against other believers, however, lies are whispered to our flesh: *your fruit isn't as shiny, your fruit isn't as fragrant, your fruit is too mushy and flavorless.* A lie is born in thinking that all trees produce the same fruit. That just isn't true.

Your relationship with Jesus Christ is unique. He produces, between you and the Holy Spirit, an exceptional fruit that only grows from *your* branches. You can be who God made you to be. We are all capable and expected to grow fruit that exhibits the fruit of the Holy Spirit. When we come together, according to God's perfect recipe, for his glory, it is truly delicious.

> *Lord, thank you that I don't need to compare my fruit to others'. You have made me with a distinct flavor that can benefit those around me when I submit myself to you. Give me the strength and confidence I need to embrace my individuality.*

Made Beautiful

He has made everything beautiful in its time.
He has also set eternity in the human heart;
yet no one can fathom what God has done
from beginning to end.

Ecclesiastes 3:11 NIV

We've probably all heard an older gentleman declare that his wife is more beautiful now than the day they married. And we likely thought, *He needs glasses.* What we fail to recognize in our outward-focused, airbrushed society, is that time really does make things beautiful. More accurately, time gives us better perspective on the true definition of beauty.

Spending time with those we love affords us a glimpse into the depth of beauty that lies within. So while the external beauty may be fading, there is a wealth of beauty inside—and *that's* the beauty the older gentleman was referring to.

God's Word says that he makes all things beautiful in his time. *All* things. Whatever situation you are facing right now, it has the potential to create beauty in you. Believe it! Perseverance, humility, grace, obedience—these are beautiful.

There's more. The beauty God creates in us cannot be fully described in human terms. There is eternal beauty beyond what we can fathom.

> *God, when I am met with challenges, help me to run to you and sit in your presence. I know that when I do, I can't help but reflect the beauty of your character. Help me to allow all that I am facing right now to be a catalyst for true beauty.*

"Come to me,
all you that are weary
and are carrying
heavy burdens,
and I will
give you rest."

MATTHEW 11:28 NRSV

The Unseen

Faith is confidence in what we hope for and
assurance about what we do not see.

Hebrews 11:1 NIV

Where does belief originate? We can look to scientific
evidence of the earth's creation by an intelligent designer,
and there are many scientific specialists who can discuss the
details passionately and convincingly.

We can read the prophecies from Scripture that also point to
the truth of God's power, presence, and passion. Then there
are scholars, preachers, and authorities who tell you about
the prophecies. The historic evidence of the existence of Jesus
Christ comes with another set of experts who can explain the
proof and compelling evidence.

Finally, we have his people: the humble followers of Jesus
who have experienced his saving grace. We were blind, but

now we can see. We were lost, and now we are found. We were dead in our sins, but now we are alive in Jesus Christ! This is all we can *know* for certain. We may not be scientists, theologians, or experts in apologetics, but we know that we were blind and God enlightened us. We were lost and God gave us a home. We were dead and he raised us from our graves and gave us hope.

What we believe is true. God created the earth. He spoke the planets, oceans, and trees into being. He imparted to the prophets details of the coming Messiah, and Jesus came and fulfilled those promises in perfect detail. But our very testimonies—our transformation from death to life—are the simple and powerful proof that what we believe is true.

> *God, it is undeniable that I am different*
> *today than I was before I knew you.*
> *Thank you for your work in my life and*
> *in the world around me.*

Walking Boldly

Let us come boldly to the throne of our
gracious God. There we will receive his
mercy, and we will find grace to help us
when we need it most.

Hebrews 4:16 NLT

We have full access to the throne of God! Is there any throne
on earth granting this much access, this little security, so
much grace? Imagine walking into Buckingham Palace,
unnoticed and unrestricted, without knocking or announcing
yourself, and pulling up a chair alongside Her Majesty, the
Queen of England.

"Hello, your Majesty. Quite the weather we're having. I was
wondering if you could give me some advice on a problem
I've been having at home. Do you have some time?"

It's bizarre and ridiculous, obviously. There are procedures to follow, etiquette, protocol for seeing royalty—not to mention the armed guards, alarms, and jail, probably.

Thankfully, there is a royal throne toward which we can walk with boldness because we have all the credentials we need. There are no guards, no necessary payments, and no barred doors. Its occupant is the God of all creation, and he is eager to help us with anything we need.

God's throne is the only throne that is worthy of our worship. Approach his throne, and shamelessly pull up a chair. He loves your company and will never send you away. Walk in boldness as you approach the throne and lift your voice to him.

Father, I come boldly to you today,
asking for grace, strength, and
guidance. You are so wise and I want
to hear what you have to say. Thank
you that I don't have to be afraid to
approach you. You care about the
smallest details of my life.

No Fear

Such love has no fear, because perfect love
expels all fear. If we are afraid, it is for fear of
punishment, and this shows that we have
not fully experienced his perfect love.

1 John 4:18 NLT

Fear rears its ugly head in lots of ways: the spider waiting
in your bathtub, the high bridge you pass going to your
favorite park, the loud noise outside your bedroom window
in the middle of the night. It can be gripping, paralyzing, or
terrifying for some. For others, it is motivation to conquer
weakness.

Those fears are mostly related to phobias, which, one could
argue, stem from basic human defense instincts. What about
the fears that keep us awake at night? The worries and
anxieties that cannot be brushed aside?

Early followers of Jesus worried about what would happen on Judgment Day. Was his death enough to cover their sins completely and guarantee their eternity in heaven? John points out their fear as one of punishment. But there isn't room for fear alongside perfect love, and if we are abiding in the love of God, then we have perfect love in us. Fear must surrender.

We must surrender as well. We must surrender to the truth that sets us free: Jesus died and is now alive—so our sin is dead and we are alive. *We are alive!* Jesus has overcome death, sin, and fear! We can live with the resurrection of Jesus in mind. We have nothing to fear and no debt to pay. Heights and spiders and enclosed spaces might still quicken our hearts, but we can rest easy in his perfect love, now and for all eternity.

God, I want to be alive with this truth.
Help me to bask in your love every
moment of the day. Fear cannot remain
when I am in your perfect love.

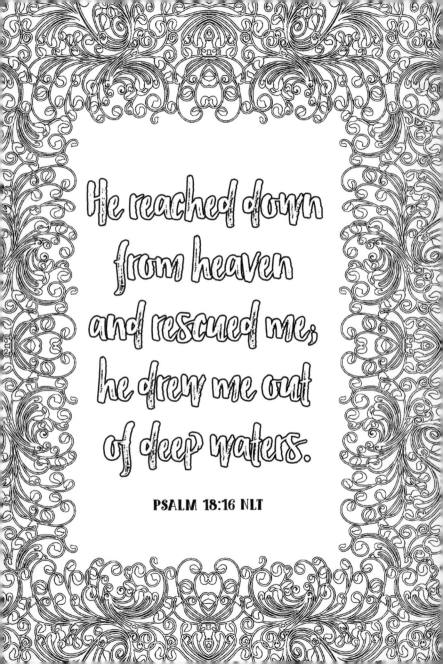

He reached down
from heaven
and rescued me;
he drew me out
of deep waters.

PSALM 18:16 NLT

Without Compromise

When troubles of any kind come your way,
consider it an opportunity for great joy. For
you know that when your faith is tested,
your endurance has a chance to grow. So
let it grow, for when your endurance is
fully developed, you will be perfect and
complete, needing nothing.

James 1:2-4 NLT

The best products are built using the best ingredients. Some companies compromise, and when trouble inevitably comes, their products suffer and they lose money. But organizations dedicated to quality without compromise build things that endure.

Oh, beloved, that our faith would be strengthened for endurance! What are we made of? Can we stand the test? Trouble is on the horizon, but we are advised to see it as an opportunity for great joy.

This isn't easy advice to follow, but in his wisdom, God gave his Word for our benefit. What would we expect him to say? *Dear children, when troubles of any kind come your way, curl up into a ball of despair for all hope is probably lost.* Of course not! God is building us to last! We would not gain blessing through hopelessness. No, he builds our faith with the highest-quality parts: hope in the promises of God's Word, humility from the grace that he has given us, and love for God who first loved us.

Built with quality, we can have great joy. Our endurance grows and we are proven perfect and complete, needing nothing.

> *God, help me not to compromise when I am tested. I want to be found lacking nothing. I want opportunities for great joy, and I accept that those opportunities come through enduring trials. Thank you for the grace you've given me to continue.*

Finding Comfort

May our Lord Jesus Christ himself and God
our Father, who loved us and by his grace
gave us eternal comfort and a wonderful
hope, comfort and strengthen you.

2 Thessalonians 2:16-17 NLT

There are so many things that we choose to comfort
ourselves with: food, entertainment, relationships, music, or
even just busyness. We'll choose anything to take our minds
off the wave of emotion that is raging inside.

It's much easier to grab a pint of chocolate ice cream, or
throw ourselves into a project, than it is to face what's really
going on. But those comforts just don't last. They are empty,
short-lived, hollow, flat.

The apostle Paul said that God is the God of *all* comfort (see 2
Corinthians 1:3). The things we use to comfort ourselves that

aren't from God are destined to fail. They can't offer the hope, peace, security, or love found in the presence of God. They can't reach into the deepest places inside us and turn our sorrows into joy.

When you choose to find your comfort in God, you will not be disappointed. He knows everything you have faced since the moment you were born, and he knows the best way to comfort you right now.

Father, I need your comfort today. I want to find the true, lasting peace that only comes from being your child and resting in your love. Be with me throughout the day and remind me of your goodness as I choose to look at all that I am blessed with.

Walking Confidently

Be my rock of refuge, to which I can always go;
give the command to save me,
for you are my rock and my fortress.
For you have been my hope, Sovereign Lord,
my confidence since my youth.

Psalm 71:3, 5 NIV

The foot traffic in the park was heavy: moms pushing strollers, joggers huffing over the trails, kids with baseball gloves and bats heading for open fields, couples meandering hand-in-hand under the leafy canopy.

Observe closely and one can tell a lot about a person. Their posture, especially, is revealing. The man on the park bench, shoulders hunched, seems discouraged. One jogger lifts her head towards the sun, hopeful, while a mother's eyes dart nervously back and forth.

It is obvious when our hopes have sunk into shifting sand; we find no peace, no comfort, and no protective fortress from distress. Our foreheads wrinkle, our steps drift, our distraught hands clasp and wring. Our confidence is lost.

What do you see when you look in the mirror? Worry lines or laugh lines? Are your eyes cloudy with anxieties or bright with possibilities? Are you hesitant or confident?

God is the rock on which you can firmly plant your hopes. Lift your eyes to the Son and walk with confidence. The sovereign Lord is the only hope and assurance you need!

> *God, so many things distract me from*
> *walking in confidence. I give them to you*
> *now and ask you to restore my hope.*

Constant in Change

A furious squall came up, and the waves broke
over the boat, so that it was nearly swamped.
Jesus was in the stern, sleeping on a cushion.
The disciples woke him and said to him,
"Teacher, don't you care if we drown?"
He got up, rebuked the wind and said to the
waves, "Quiet! Be still!" Then the wind died
down and it was completely calm. He said to
his disciples, "Why are you so afraid? Do you
still have no faith?"

Mark 4:37-40 NIV

It takes time to adjust to changing situations. Sailors need
time to get their "sea legs," mountain climbers rest in order
to adjust their lungs to altitude changes, and scuba divers
surface slowly to regulate pressure. Even adjusting to
daylight-savings can take some time.

During their time with Jesus in his ministry on earth, the disciples had to adjust quickly to radical situations. A daughter was raised from the dead, a boy's meager lunch multiplied to feed a crowd of 5,000, a demon was cast into a herd of pigs that threw themselves off a cliff. Could they have woken up in the morning and sufficiently prepared for such things? Then one day, they get in a boat and their limited faith is tested.

It seems as though the disciples never really adjusted to the unpredictability of life with Jesus. Have you? If they struggled while in his very presence, how can we have faith to walk confidently into the unknown? We have his Word and the assurance that his presence is all we need; he is constant in the face of change.

As his daughter, you are always in his presence. No matter what you are facing, you can walk confidently. It may take some time, but he is prepared for everything and he will prepare you too.

God, I admit that change makes me feel uneasy. Help me to trust you in the storm. You are steady and you do not change. I believe in that promise today.

Finding Contentment

I have learned in whatever situation I am to
be content. I know how to be brought low,
and I know how to abound. In any and every
circumstance, I have learned the secret of
facing plenty and hunger, abundance and
need. I can do all things through him who
strengthens me.

Philippians 4:11-13, ESV

Paul shares with us his beautiful secret, which followers of
Jesus Christ have been surviving on since it was penned,
sealed, and delivered to the Church at Philippi. We are
promised a life of persecution, sacrifice, and rejection.

The key to unlocking contentment amidst the trials is in
trusting that your needs have been met. Trust eliminates the
spectrum between "life is good" and "life is bad." With trust,
all life lived in the strength of Jesus is contentment. All life

is satisfaction. Everything is a fulfillment of his promise that following him is all we need.

Contentment grows in the midst of discomfort. Joy is found despite the trouble around every corner. A life of faith prospers amid the ruins. Find contentment in God. Comfort is found when you trust in your Father for everything. You don't need the trappings and the shimmer of the temporary. Whether you have everything or nothing, you can trade it all for the eternal.

God strengthens us to endure these worldly wanderings for the hope and promise of our eternal existence.

Father, I want to believe that you truly meet my every need. Your ways are perfect and good, and I believe you for contentment today.

On the Right Path

*Make me to know your ways, O L*ORD*;*
teach me your paths.
*Good and upright is the L*ORD*;*
therefore he instructs sinners in the way.
He leads the humble in what is right,
and teaches the humble his way.
*All the paths of the L*ORD *are steadfast love and*
faithfulness,
for those who keep his covenant and his
testimonies.

Psalm 25:4, 8-10 ESV

GPS has nothing on God. We use satellites because we want to know where we are going, how long it will take to get there, and how many miles we will travel on our journey. Our lives, however, don't have coordinates recognized by modern-day digital guides.

Only our loving and faithful God leads us in the direction we really need to go. Not only that, but he teaches us his ways as we walk with him. He *instructs sinners* who humbly learn to be *good and upright*.

The world's guidance can instruct you to take a left—directly into a murky pond. Satellites aren't as accurate as God's perfect instructions. By keeping his covenant and testimonies, we stay on the right path.

With God, both the journey and the destination are worth the effort. We are transformed by travel; we are reinvented by a loving and faithful leader. When mapping out a travel itinerary, won't we look for a path of steadfast love and faithfulness? When we keep his covenant and his testimonies, we receive the promises he gives us in his Word. Trust God to keep you on the right path.

God there have been many times I've taken a wrong turn in my life. I see your faithfulness even in those moments. I humble myself today and ask for your help. Thank you for coming to get me and guiding me back to the right path.

I will say
of the Lord,
"He is my refuge
and my fortress,
my God,
in whom I trust."

PSALM 91:2 NIV

Courage

May he give you the power to accomplish all
the good things our faith prompts you to do.

2 Thessalonians 1:11 NLT

Courage is often associated with acts of bravery that defy
typical human experience: running through flames to save a
child, jumping in a raging river to pull someone to shore, or
chasing down a thief to retrieve a stolen purse.

But courage doesn't always look so heroic. Courage is
standing your ground when you feel like running; it's saying
yes to something you feel God is telling you to do even when
you aren't sure that you can do it.

Courage can be telling someone you don't want to hear their
negative thoughts about other people. It can be sharing
your testimony with a room full of people—or with one.
Sometimes it takes courage just to leave your house.

When we place our trust and hope in God, he will give us the courage we need to do the tasks he wants us to do. If that includes doing something *heroic,* great! But let's not underestimate the importance of walking courageously in the small things as well.

Father, there are a number of situations in my life right now that require me to be brave. I believe that even as I take the first step, you are with me and you will give me the courage to finish what I start.

Depending On God

Be strong and courageous. Do not be afraid
or terrified...for the LORD your God goes with
you; he will never leave you
nor forsake you.

Deuteronomy 31:6 NIV

Death and taxes. They say those are the two things we can
depend on in life. Of course they don't mention the neighbor
who fails to return the cordless drill (again), the empty fuel
light blinking when you're late for work (again), and the
spontaneous yet cheerful visitor ringing the doorbell when
you're still in your pajamas at 3pm (again). Unpredictability is
something else we can depend on!

Through every unpredictable situation, through all
disappointments, delays, and disruptions, we can cling even
more confidently to the faithfulness of God. He is the one
solid rock on which we can firmly stand. He is steadfast and
loyal, asking us to trust in his promises.

God commands that we not be afraid or terrified; if it weren't possible, he wouldn't ask it of us. He guarantees that he will always be with us, no matter where we go. If it weren't true, he wouldn't promise it.

Life will be shaky and unpredictable—*that* you can count on! By the grace of God you will never have to endure it alone. There is nothing that will cause him to change his dependable ways. Death and taxes will come. So will life's unpredictable twists and turns. But do not be afraid; God is by your side. You can depend on him.

Lord, as I think about the areas in my life
that are unpredictable, I am encouraged
by your faithfulness. You will always be
near me. Thank you that I can cling to you
when all else is shaking.

Determined to Stay the Course

> Do you not know that in a race all the
> runners run, but only one gets the prize?
> Run in such a way as to get the prize.
> Everyone who competes in the games goes
> into strict training. They do it to get a crown
> that will not last, but we do it to get a crown
> that will last forever.

1 Corinthians 9:24-25 NIV

Runners have honed the evasive skill of self-control. They have the willpower to overcome physical pain and exhaustion. They have the stamina to push past throbbing muscles, breathlessness, and lead feet. They have, first and foremost, the ability to follow through with the plan.

Running may be on the schedule, but, like anyone else, runners have to actually put running shoes on and move their feet along the pavement. Sure, it's more comfortable on the couch. Yes, it's easier to walk, and many runners would rather get together with friends. But they have committed to the plan. And the plan says, *Get dressed, lace up your shoes, and get on the course. Now.*

So they do. This is the only difference between runners and non-runners. And it is the only difference between believers and non-believers. Believers in Jesus Christ have determined to stay the course because it's what is asked of us. Non-believers are also running through life, but their direction changes with the wind.

Running this race is the greatest challenge of your life. It requires self-control, motivation, and stamina. It requires submission to the training: saying yes every day to getting dressed, lacing up your shoes, and staying on the course. Determine to run the race so that you will win!

God, show me what is hindering me
from putting my running shoes on and
hitting the track. Help me to see life
through your eyes, and let it motivate
me to stay the course.

Don't worry about anything; instead, pray about everything.

PHILIPPIANS 4:6 NLT

Wholly Devoted

He alone is your God, the only one who
is worthy of your praise, the one who has
done these mighty miracles that you have
seen with your own eyes.

Deuteronomy 10:21 NLT

At the unveiling of the city's newest skyscraper, crowds
gathered to celebrate the feat of architecture and
engineering, commerce, and creativity. Sunlight poured
onto the observation deck as a city official cut the yellow
dedication ribbon. Behind him were some of the many
construction workers, designers, and engineers whose
imagination, insight, and expertise contributed to making
mere drawings a reality.

Only one expert can truly take credit for the building's
inception—the architect. That is who conceived of the
shape, size, and details of the building. He intimately knows

the building: inside and out. But everyone reaches for the spotlight. The architect is lost in the noise and clamor for glory.

You know this architect. He is your designer: the one responsible for your soaring heights and multitude of blessings. *He alone is your God.* Have you singled him out for glory? *The only one who is worthy of your praise.* Have you heralded to him a song of thanksgiving?

The mighty miracles of your life are his careful design, plain for all to see. You can be wholly devoted to God, the architect of the strong, graceful, beautiful tower that is *you*.

> *Father, there are so many things I am thankful for in life. Thank you for your hand of blessing in the big and little things. I offer all of those blessings back to you today and honor you for your work in my life.*

Head Held High

My thoughts are not your thoughts,
neither are your ways my ways, declares the LORD.
For as the heavens are higher than the earth,
so are my ways higher than your ways
and my thoughts than your thoughts.

Isaiah 55:8-9 ESV

In times of war, army strategists benefit from high vantage points. Looking upon the battlefield from above is the best way to formulate strategies for their troops. Before the use of satellite equipment and heat-sensing radar, views were limited to ground level, forcing the use of maps and spies to predict enemy movement and position men. After their invention, hot-air balloons were used by generals in battle to accurately determine the locations of enemy troops.

In the same way, our lives benefit from a higher viewpoint. When we rise above our circumstances and see life, not from our own anxious, urgent, sometimes overwhelming perspective, but from God's, life's battles become less intimidating as eternity's promises rise into view.

God has plans for your life, but sometimes they are hard to see. The day-to-day defeats of life consume us and we struggle to confidently lift our head above the fray. When this happens, remember his high thoughts and ways, and believe that he will lead you.

Walk with your head held high, knowing that he sees everything that surrounds you. Trust him. He will lead you safely to the other side.

> *God, all of my decisions require a higher*
> *vantage point because I want to view*
> *them with your perspective. Lead me*
> *in your perfect way throughout each*
> *day. Give me your heart for people and*
> *situations so I make decisions that are*
> *based on your thoughts and ways*

Finding Encouragement

I want you to save me Lord,
I love your teachings.
Let me live so I can praise you,
and let your laws help me.

Psalm 119:174-175 NCV

There is wonder to be found in snowflakes, raindrops, and even strange bugs. Though we often don't love the idea of encountering too many of those things, if we stop and look, if we allow ourselves to really *see* what is there, it's pretty amazing.

The same can be true of God's Word. It may be displayed in various forms and places throughout our homes, schools, work places, or church buildings, but if we don't stop to really drink in the words that are there, we can miss the rich blessing behind them.

When we believe that God wants to encourage us through his Word, we will no doubt find encouragement in it—because God intended it to be used for that purpose!

Don't gloss over the beauty and depth of his Word. It's the only Word that carries the richness of eternity.

God, help me to find my encouragement in your Word. Thank you that you have given it to me for that very reason. Your Word is full of goodness and life. It is the very essence of truth, and I praise you for it.

One thing
I ask from the Lord,
this only do I seek:
that I may dwell
in the house of the Lord
all the days of my life,
to gaze on the beauty
of the Lord
and to seek him
in his temple.

PSALM 27:4 NIV

Enduring Hardship

Consider it pure joy… whenever you face
trials of many kinds, because you know
that the testing of your faith produces
perseverance. Let perseverance finish
its work so that you may be mature and
complete, not lacking anything.

James 1:2-4 NIV

Creating a diamond is, for the transforming coal, a long and
painful process. Simple carbon undergoes an immense refining
pressure that produces a wholly new creation. We might just
see a cloudy rock at this stage, but there is another refining
step to be taken. After the stone-cutter does his work, a precise
shining diamond emerges: magnificent, glittering, brilliant.

When we endure hardship, the long and painful process can
seem unfair. To the mother with terminal cancer, it seems
excessive. To the abandoned wife, it seems unjust. To the
orphaned daughter, it seems cruel.

But our life stories are written by a compassionate Creator who is crafting a masterpiece. He is refining us, like the diamond, into something entirely beyond our imagination. And we can rejoice in the beauty he is creating. You may not see it now, but it's coming soon.

The pressure and the pain happen first. The coal cannot avoid this part. But it is the choice, after so much pain, to become more than clear rocks—to see our beauty and joy shimmering beneath the surface—and submit to the shaping and polishing of God's skilled and loving hands. Let the pressure not be for nothing. Know that you can endure hardship and emerge stronger and brighter than ever.

God, thank you that the painful
processes I endure are for a purpose.
You desire to see beauty emerge from
the hardship. I trust you through the
process and allow you to have your way
in my life.

Believe God for More

By faith Abraham obeyed when he was
called to go out to a place that he was to
receive as an inheritance. And he went out,
not knowing where he was going.

Hebrews 11:8 ESV

Is it a surprise to learn that God can give you all that your
heart desires and more? Is it a surprise to know that our
human expectations are so limited that they cannot even
begin to imagine the fullness of joy in Jesus Christ? We have
expectations of glory, but God urges us to come up higher, to
stretch our faith. Are we ready for more?

We have been given a very high calling and we cannot
achieve it without some exercise. Like it or not, we must get a
little uncomfortable, a little sore, a little sweaty. Maybe a lot.
But we are capable of so much more than we know. We are
braver than we believe. Stronger than we seem. Smarter than
we think.

Believing God for more first requires commitment to the challenge; following God into the unknown is strenuous on both mind and strength, and without commitment we'll inevitably give up. It pushes the boundaries of faith, asking that we put aside our limited expectations and believe God's promise of joy. And just when we think we can't endure any more, God reveals the view from the mountaintop and all the strain is suddenly worth it.

We realize that the exercise itself is its own reward; the challenges are worth every drop of sweat and every moment of pain. With expectations stretched, faith is strengthened for God to use us in greater measure. We are ready for a higher climb to a greater height where we find more astonishing joy.

God, I want to believe you for more. I stretch my expectations to believe you for even greater things in my life. I know you will not disappoint me. In you I find incredible joy and strength.

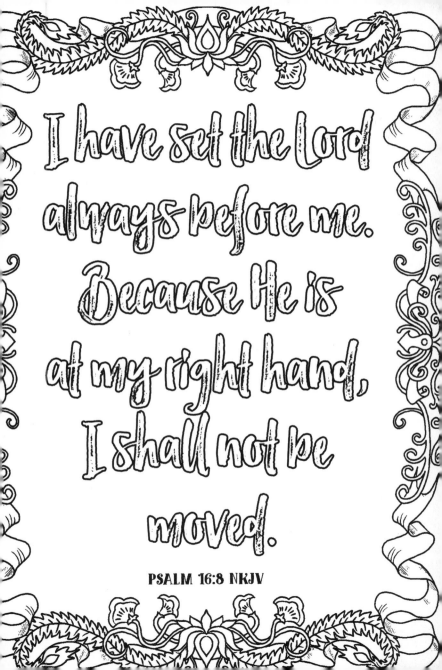

I have set the Lord always before me. Because He is at my right hand, I shall not be moved.

PSALM 16:8 NKJV

Where He Leads Me

With weeping they shall come,
and with pleas for mercy I will lead them back,
I will make them walk by brooks of water,
in a straight path in which they shall not stumble,
for I am a father to Israel.

Jeremiah 31:9 ESV

The journey of the believer is a lifelong pilgrimage that ends not at a religious temple or city, but in the kingdom of heaven. Our journey's hardships, sacrifices, and struggles are part of our displacement, and they won't end until eternity. Wherever the path leads, we follow. However long and dusty the road, we press on. No matter what storms lay ahead, we continue. With determined steps we press on toward our destination until we are welcomed home.

Before we began this pilgrimage, we were broken, dead in sin, and weeping from our wounds. Our merciful God redeemed us and brought us up out of the mire. It may not always seem like it, but this path he has set us on is full of restoration, nourishment, steadfastness, and love.

The many steps of our pilgrimage are not walked alone, but alongside one who never gets lost, tired, or afraid. God knows we were confused and alone for a long time, so he personally leads us. He knows we are thirsty, so there are sanctuaries along the way. He knows we were bruised and broken while stumbling along our old pathways, so he navigates a straight route for our safety.

God is a good Father and you can trust his leadership. Go wherever he leads, beloved. Your pilgrimage is a long and beautiful journey, and it's worth every step.

> *Lord God, lead me in this season of my*
> *life. I trust you enough to say that I will*
> *go wherever you lead me. I know that*
> *even when it involves struggle, it will*
> *be for my best. You will show me the*
> *reward of my obedience in due time.*

The Faithfulness of God

Let us draw near to God with a sincere heart
and with the full assurance that faith brings,
having our hearts sprinkled to cleanse us
from a guilty conscience and having our
bodies washed with pure water. Let us hold
unswervingly to the hope we profess, for he
who promised is faithful.

Hebrews 10:22-23 NIV

God is good and he knows all of your needs. He is faithful and
he longs to show more of his glory and beauty.

God, show us more of you! Show us how much you can do
through our fellowship and communion. Show us how far your
faithful hands can reach and how much love they will pour
out upon your Bride. Prepare our hearts to say yes to your call.
Clear a path and make a way so we can fulfill your plans.

We will not lose heart, God! We trust in your faithfulness. We love you fully, like children chasing after joy. Our love is pleasing to you, because you delight in your children. You sing over your children, notes and refrains here and there as we walk the earth, waiting for you. One day, your song will be complete, and when we hear its fullness, we will run to you!

Until that day, we trust in your faithfulness. *We hold unswervingly to the hope we profess* because we have *the full assurance that faith brings;* our hearts are cleansed and we are pure.

Lord, your faithfulness has been demonstrated in my life in so many ways. Thank you for your sacrifice that has cleansed me and given me hope.

I Am Forgiven

"Her sins—and they are many—have been
forgiven, so she has shown me much love.
But a person who is forgiven little shows
only little love." Then Jesus said to the
woman, "Your sins are forgiven."

Luke 7:47-48 NLT

It can be so hard to trust in complete forgiveness—so hard
to trust that all of the horrible, shameful, repulsive sins of the
past are known by Jesus and yet fully forgiven.

If you were the repentant prostitute sitting at the feet of Jesus,
would you believe? Could you confidently listen to your sins,
listed in detail for all to hear, and say, "Amen! I have been
forgiven! Yes, even of that, hallelujah!"

This woman's sins were known to all, and rather than hiding
in shame away from the world, she sought Jesus because

she believed in his forgiveness. He would not turn from her in disgust, shut her out, or reject her. By faith, she was completely accepted, loved, and redeemed.

The Pharisee's rebuke of her presence seems so heartless; doesn't he understand that no one could possibly have greater reason to rejoice than this woman? No offering of oil, poured out on the redeemer's feet, could be more pleasing than the one from these humble and grateful hands. Jesus loves the heights of her gratitude; they are equal to the depths from which she has been saved.

> *God, I can relate to the burden of this woman. I can relate to her pain and shame. I understand her deep and desperate longing to worship at your feet. Thank you that I am forgiven— fully, completely, and lovingly, and you have called me worthy to worship you.*

God Is Good

You are a chosen people. You are royal priests,
a holy nation, God's very own possession. As
a result, you can show others the goodness of
God, for he called you out of the darkness into
his wonderful light.

1 Peter 2:9 NLT

God is good and he makes all things good. Evil is the absence
of God's goodness. Like light and darkness, goodness cannot
exist in the same place as evil. The world, however, often
seems to exist in shades of gray. Light and darkness tangle
together to become something indecipherable, and the
resulting shadows breed uncertainty.

Politicians, activists, and corporations love uncertainty
because it encourages a second look at what once seemed
certain. What society believed was good has shifted, but God
never shifts. His goodness is certain.

Let's begin with that. *He is good.* Now, decipher the light from the darkness, the good from the evil, knowing that God doesn't change and is always good. He is good in unemployment, in sickness, in despair, in bankruptcy, in another's betrayal, even when it seems like darkness is all around.

He called you out of the darkness into his wonderful light. You belong to him, you are chosen, and you can believe in his goodness.

Walk in his wonderful light. God is good and he redeemed you from your sin. He never leaves you. He has reserved a place for you in his kingdom. He is light, and darkness cannot exist in the light.

> *God, I believe you are good. There*
> *are so many areas in my life that give*
> *testimony to your goodness. Thank you*
> *for choosing to share your abundance*
> *and blessing with me.*

Grace That Is Sufficient

God is so rich in mercy, and he loved us
so much, that even though we were dead
because of our sins, he gave us life when
he raised Christ from the dead. (It is only by
God's grace that you have been saved!)…
God saved you by his grace when you
believed. And you can't take credit for this; it
is a gift from God. Salvation is not a reward
for the good things we have done, so none
of us can boast about it.

Ephesians 2:4-5, 8-9 NLT

There is no greater education in the amazing grace of God
than his own words. When the impact of his grace has saved
you, these words have a particularly powerful and humbling
effect. We have done nothing, yet we have everything. We
were dead, but now we have life. We didn't pay with money,
flesh, or enslavement. We just believed.

Because of his amazing grace, and because we believe this truth, we have everything we need. Our eternity is established. Is there anything else we require? We have a salvation that cannot be lost, stolen, forfeited, or forgotten. And God's grace for us will never fail, fade, or diminish.

We cannot boast in our salvation, but we can sing praises from the rafters for this amazing gift. Sing long and loud, for grace is the one and only gift we will ever need. And we can share it, without losing an ounce of our portion. It multiplies over and over, as long as we are willing to give it away.

Know beyond a shadow of doubt that his grace is sufficient for you. It has been from the moment you believed!

Thank you, God, for the undeserved
gift of grace you have given me. I fail
time and time again, and yet your grace
remains sufficient. You have saved me
and have given me life and hope.
I am blessed!

Seek
his will
in all you do,
and he will
show you
which path
to take.

PROVERBS 3:6 NLT

All of Life's Blessings

Let your roots grow down into him, and let
your lives be built on him. Then your faith will
grow strong in the truth you were taught, and
you will overflow with thankfulness.

Colossians 2:7 NLT

Gratitude makes a lovely countenance. When our cups
overflow with gratitude, there isn't room for bitterness or
criticism. Gratitude pushes away judgement and disdain and
makes room for joy and grace.

People walking in gratitude make very pleasant company.
Their overflow of thankfulness blesses everyone, from families
and friends to the people in line with them at the post office.

What a testimony to God's goodness! When we have an
attitude of thanks, we confirm that we have been blessed.
And beloved, we have indeed been greatly blessed. Beyond

material blessings, beyond the blessing of health and home, beyond even the blessing of family and friends, we have the immeasurable blessing of faith.

By faith, we build our lives on the Word of God. By faith, we grow strong and learn the truth of God. By faith, we *overflow with thankfulness*. Our thankfulness is a gift back to God.

Let your life be a testimony of gratitude. Let the aroma of your thankfulness touch the senses of everyone around you—a sweet perfume of God's faithfulness to you. He has blessed you and it is right that you would overflow with praise! Root yourself in God, build your life on him, and watch your faith strengthen.

Father, I pray that my thankfulness
would overflow to the furthest reaches
of my life. That it would be contagious
and compelling, reflecting your glory.

Walking Honorably

The name of the Lord Jesus will be honored
because of the way you live, and you will
be honored along with him. This is all made
possible because of the grace of our God
and Lord, Jesus Christ.

2 Thessalonians 1:12 NLT

Honor awards are usually given to those who achieve
excellence in specific fields. People are honored for their
performance in musical, athletic, academic, and professional
arenas. Some are honored for their exceptional bravery or
intelligence. And rightly so. But if honor is given only for
excellent achievement, how on earth can we be considered
honorable with our less-than-impressive abilities?

The secret to living a life that honors God is found in
depending heavily on his grace to cover us. We keep it simple.
We do what we know is right, and we don't do what we know

is wrong. We don't compromise. We don't chase after the shiny honor awards of the world. And when we get it wrong, we humbly admit our failure, accept God's forgiveness, and keep walking the narrow road.

It's crazy to think that we are even capable of bringing honor to God through our lives. We're so *human*, and he's so *perfect*. But that's precisely it—we *aren't* able to walk honorably on our own. We can't achieve the excellence standard required. It's only by his grace that we are considered worthy of his honor award.

> *God, help me to rightly evaluate the honor awards I seek after. I want to bring honor to your name and your kingdom. Thank you for your grace that makes this possible.*

The Lord will work out his plans for my life for your faithful love, O Lord, endures forever.

PSALM 138:8 NLT

Humble Walk

Get rid of all evil behavior. Be done with all deceit, hypocrisy, jealousy, and all unkind speech. Like newborn babies, you must crave pure spiritual milk so that you will grow into a full experience of salvation. Cry out for this nourishment, now that you have had a taste of the Lord's kindness.

1 Peter 2:1-3 NLT

Evil behaviors are rooted in ungodly pride. When we come to faith in Jesus Christ, we must become like him, a humble servant, shedding our pride and living a life of honesty, integrity, contentment, and kindness. The path to this life begins with humility.

Nothing is more dependent, more completely humble, than a newborn baby. A precious life, whose only hope is a loving, kind, capable provider, lays waiting for nourishment.

If placed in your arms, you alone become solely responsible for meeting her needs, even if all you can do is hand her back to her mother. But while in your arms, she humbly relies on *you* to provide.

In our spiritual infancy, we are completely humble and fully dependent on God's kindness. Our meals consist of spiritual food; putting off our old lives of sin, crying out for goodness and tasting the pure love of God. Then our humble path continues, though the climb gets tougher.

Through it all, keep the posture of Jesus Christ your servant, who came to lose his life so you could gain the abundant, eternal, glorious life in the kingdom of heaven. Walk in humility and grow in servanthood.

> *God, show me what behaviors I need to adjust to ensure that I am walking in humility. I submit to you and thank you for your example of servanthood.*

Find Inspiration

The word of God is alive and powerful. It is
sharper than the sharpest two-edged sword,
cutting between soul and spirit, between
joint and marrow. It exposes our innermost
thoughts and desires.

Hebrews 4:12 NLT

Have you ever opened your Bible to a random page, begun to
read, and been amazed that the Scripture passage is perfectly
appropriate for that exact season of your life? Then at church
your pastor uses the same verse as the basis for a sermon.
While driving a few days later, a worship song's lyrics match
up to your life, again. It's like God has a spotlight on you and is
aligning the world around you to encourage, direct, or teach
you wherever you are. His Word is truly *alive and powerful*!

The Word of God is a marvelously insightful gift. He gave it for
our edification, education, and inspiration. Whatever we are

going through, the Word of God holds the answer. Whether we are running away from God or toward him, whether we are rejoicing or mourning, however confused or secure we feel, God's Word holds the solution.

Reading his Word *exposes our innermost thoughts and desires.* Sound uncomfortable? A bit too vulnerable? We don't usually like feeling uncomfortable, and reading God's commandments brings conviction. Child of God, count this as a blessing!

God shines a spotlight on areas to inspire us toward greater submission to him. When we are submitted, we become more and more like Jesus. And that is what we really want, right? Find inspiration in God's Word! It is a powerful gift that helps you learn, grow, and believe.

> *God, help me pay attention to the*
> *Scriptures that continue to crop up.*
> *I want to listen to what you are saying to*
> *me by pondering those verses.*
> *I know your living Word can have a*
> *direct impact on my life as I submit*
> *myself to it.*

You will keep in perfect peace those whose minds are steadfast, because they trust in you.

ISAIAH 26:3 NIV

Integrity

Teach me your decrees, O Lord;
I will keep them to the end.
Give me understanding
and I will obey your instructions;
I will put them into practice
with all my heart.
Make me walk along the path
of your commands,
for that is where my happiness is found.

Psalm 119:33-35 NLT

Adventurous Hollywood tales of heroes have little in common with reality, except, perhaps, the hero. Heroes really do exist. They serve us coffee, or walk their dogs down our street. Maybe you are a hero. It doesn't take much really, just being in the right place at the right time. And, of course, doing the right thing. This is what sets a hero apart: a hero does the right thing.

Heroes put aside their own desires and interests. They have integrity, which means they do what most people wouldn't take the time, risk, or effort to do.

David's psalm reads like an oath, a decree for heroes everywhere, spoken as a promise to uphold the integrity of God's goodness and righteousness. *Place your left hand on the Bible, raise your right hand, and repeat after me...*

How can you be a hero? How can you be a woman of integrity? By learning God's commands and keeping them, asking for wisdom and committing to obedience, vowing devotion *with all your heart*, and submitting to walking God's path because it leads to joy. With God, you are always in the right place at the right time.

> *Father, I want to be someone who lives with integrity. Help me choose to do the right thing even when it isn't the popular thing. Give me opportunities to share your love with the people around me.*

God Is Just

I will proclaim the name of the LORD;
ascribe greatness to our God!
"The Rock, his work is perfect,
for all his ways are justice.
A God of faithfulness and without iniquity,
just and upright is he."

Deuteronomy 32:3-4 ESV

Being a judge is a weighty calling; if you've ever had to judge a children's art competition, you might understand. Lovingly crafted, covered in heavy-handed brush strokes, glitter, and smiling stick figures, the smudged papers are held below smiling, expectant faces. *Which one is the best?*

Could anyone choose a winner, and at the same time create a loser? More than one adult has exclaimed, "I just can't choose, they're all so wonderful!" Truly, being a judge is a calling for God alone.

Thankfully, God is great and perfect—two qualities you want in a judge. *All his ways are justice*, he is faithful and *without iniquity*. He alone is qualified to judge mankind. He alone will bring about justice with his mighty hand, and it will be eternal. Because he is faithful and without wickedness, we can rest without worry.

Winners and losers will be declared when God comes to judge. There won't be any hesitation or argument. God has seen all the world's injustice and his judgement will be poured out. Have faith in that, but in this as well: *his work is perfect.* His works of compassion, love, healing, and grace are perfect. And his ways of justice are perfect. This isn't true of us, but it is true of him, and he will make everything right one day.

> *God, sometimes I find it difficult to wait*
> *for your judgment. Help me to trust that*
> *you will rule justly in your time.*
> *I don't want to take situations into my*
> *own hands and figure them out. I want*
> *you to have your way at the right time.*

Fully Loved

Can anything ever separate us from Christ's love? Does it mean he no longer loves us if we have trouble or calamity, or are persecuted, or hungry, or destitute, or in danger, or threatened with death? (As the Scriptures say, "For your sake we are killed every day; we are being slaughtered like sheep.") No, despite all these things, overwhelming victory is ours through Christ, who loved us.

Romans 8:35-37 NLT

It's likely that we misunderstand, miscalculate, and misinterpret God's amazing love for us because we have nothing quite like it on earth. We get glimpses of it, and indeed we are only capable of loving by any degree because he first loved us, but nothing fully captures God's love. Nothing perfectly embodies his delight; nothing exactly mirrors his infatuation or faithfully interprets his depth of devotion. We fall remarkably short of his marvelous love.

No question, earthly love makes mistakes. Our love has limits, holds grudges, grows cold, and loses patience. Our love is blended, inextricably, with our flesh and all its capacity for sin. Human love is a faint whispered echo of the jubilant chorus of love sung out to us by God in all his parts. We can be glad he put it in written form—a love letter to his beloved—so we can carry it with us.

When you feel any shadow of a doubt about how greatly and completely God loves you, you only have to open your love letter to be reminded. You cannot be separated from his love. Unlike human love, God's has no limit, always forgives, never cools, and is steadfast.

Read your love letter and believe its promise: you are fully loved by God!

> *Thank you, God, for your Word which*
> *reminds me of your deep love for me.*
> *I reflect on those words of love today.*
> *Nothing can separate me from your love*
> *and for that I am so grateful.*

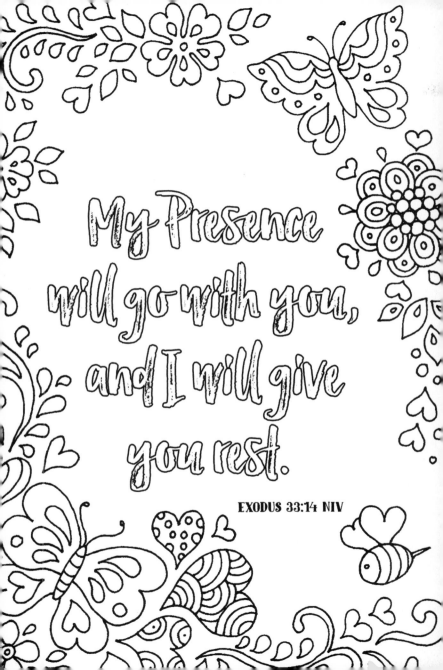

My Presence will go with you, and I will give you rest.

EXODUS 33:14 NIV

I Will Not Walk Away

"All the bridesmaids got up and prepared their lamps. Then the five foolish ones asked the others, 'Please give us some of your oil because our lamps are going out.'
But the others replied, 'We don't have enough for all of us. Go to a shop and buy some for yourselves.'
But while they were gone to buy oil, the bridegroom came. Then those who were ready went in with him to the marriage feast, and the door was locked."

Matthew 25:7-10 NLT

In the days leading up to Jesus' return, many believers will walk away. The ones who are unprepared for the pain, suffering, and sacrifice of those days will walk away from the truth. Their faith, under severe testing, will falter. Their lamps will go out.

This warning is for all believers. We hope that we will stand strong in the face of evil, but we cannot know how long and desperate the season of Christ's return will be. If even Peter, who walked alongside Jesus and loved him dearly, could deny him three times in one night long ago, then how can we know what we will do during the long night that is to come?

Begin filling your lamp with the oil of faith now, so that in the hour of Christ's return you will not walk away because of your emptiness. Only by faith will you make it through the night; faith is the oil that keeps the lamp lit.

Our perseverance in the age of Christ's return depends on our preparation. Have you stored up enough oil for that long night? Or will you have to walk away, unprepared, before the bridegroom's return? By faith and faith alone, you will not walk away!

> *Father, I want to fill my lamp and as many vessels as I can with the oil of faith. I anticipate a long night that ends with your triumphant return! Though there will be trials and testing of patience, I want to be ready when you come.*

My First Love

I know you are enduring patiently and
bearing up for my name's sake, and you
have not grown weary. But I have this
against you, that you have abandoned the
love you had at first. Remember therefore
from where you have fallen; repent, and do
the works you did at first.

Revelation 2:3-5 ESV

All we need is you, Lord. What can the world offer us that will
not perish? What can the world give that can withstand God's
refining fire? When we are tested, everything else will fall away.
Only our love for him will remain. Our salvation cannot be stolen
from us. God's love for us cannot be quenched. What, then, takes
our eyes away from his faithful gaze?

Loving God is a *choice* we make, over and over again, because
our hearts are flesh. He holds the universe and everyone on

earth; we can scarcely be trusted to hold hot coffee without burning someone. We are fickle and we forget who it was that saved us, who it was that gave us a hope and a future. We have *abandoned the love we had at first.*

But it's not too late. Remember the early days of your walk with Jesus? The way your eyes were opened to understanding, how your heart was broken in love, your arms were lifted in praise, and your knees bent in repentance? God misses that. He misses the desperation you had for him, the focused time you spent in his Word, and the joy you found in prayer.

God's love has not diminished; you can keep him as your first love.

*God, I want you to be my first love.
I choose now and every day to
remember the love I had for you when I
first believed and I want to live as I did
then. You are all I need.*

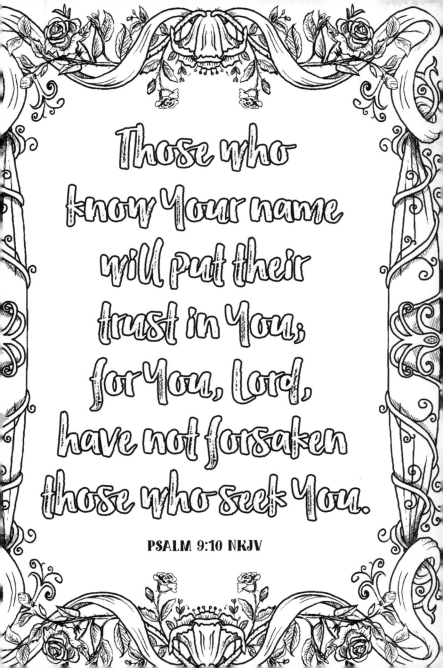

Those who know Your name will put their trust in You; for You, Lord, have not forsaken those who seek You.

PSALM 9:10 NKJV

God's Timing

We are saved by trusting. And trusting
means looking forward to getting
something we don't yet have—for a man
who already has something doesn't need to
hope and trust that he will get it. But if we
must keep trusting God for something that
hasn't happened yet, it teaches us to wait
patiently and confidently.

Romans 8:24-25 TLB

It's hard to wait for, well, anything. We can have almost
anything we want immediately. Sometimes even waiting
longer than two days to receive our order in the mail seems
way too long.

We can gain some great perspective when we think about
how life was lived hundreds or even thousands of years ago.
Mail took months to travel, items were all made to order, and

food was only delivered to your doorway if it accompanied out-of-town guests who were planning on staying for months. We have become pretty impatient, haven't we?

It's hard to wait for God's timing. Even when we are waiting for *good* things, we think we shouldn't have to wait for long. Going on a missions trip, starting a job in ministry, leading a small group, marrying the right person—doesn't God want those things for us sooner rather than later? If we don't act now, we might miss out!

Trusting in God's timing means you believe that God won't let an opportunity slip by unless it's not one he wants you to experience. Maybe he doesn't want it for you now, or maybe you're not supposed to have it at all. Can you be okay with that?

> *God, I admit that it's hard to trust you with*
> *timing. I want everything immediately.*
> *Help me to believe that you know the*
> *perfect timing for every area of my life.*
> *I won't miss out on anything except*
> *trouble if I trust you completely*
> *and move with your motion.*

Extended Hand

The LORD directs the steps of the godly.
He delights in every detail of their lives.
Though they stumble, they will never fall,
for the LORD holds them by the hand.

Psalm 37:23-24 NLT

Holding hands is a simple but beautiful act. Two people choose to join together, leading, following, or walking as equals. We might hold hands with a child to cross the street, to help an aging stranger off the bus, or to embrace even the smallest part of our beloved while strolling through the park. We grasp hands for a moment and offer safety, kindness, or affection.

Can you imagine God's hand extended to those who put their faith in him? Surely his sons and daughters need the spiritual comfort, guidance, and fellowship of God's hand more than any other. And we can be certain that God delights in extending his hand to us as well.

The world extends an enticing but dangerous hand. It can offer comfort, guidance, and fellowship. But it can also offer anxiety, burdens, and loneliness.

Take comfort in God's kindness: he is a caring Father and he leads rightly. We cannot fall when we follow his lead because his loving grip will never let us go. As a child trusts the hand that leads them safely across the busy street, so can we trust God. He is gentle, thoughtful, and compassionate, delighting over you.

God, thank you for your hand of kindness
extended gently toward me. I say yes to
walking alongside you through the ups
and downs of life. I want you to be my
guide and my comfort.

Garment of Praise

Enter his gates with thanksgiving,
and his courts with praise.
Give thanks to him, bless his name.
For the LORD is good;
his steadfast love endures forever,
and his faithfulness to all generations.

Psalm 100:4-5 NRSV

Have you ever looked into a child's grumpy face and demanded that they don't smile? Even the most stubborn child can often be coaxed out of their funk by a few tickles or funny faces. Unfortunately, the same can't be said for adults. Imagine trying to change the attitude of a crotchety woman with the same method. The picture is somewhat ridiculous.

When life's situations get us down, and all around us is dark and depressing, it takes a great deal of faith to choose praise. But often that's the only thing that can really pull us out of those dark moments.

When we choose to thank God for his goodness and grace, we can't help but see life in a more positive light. As we praise God, our focus shifts from ourselves to him.

God doesn't only deserve our praise when life is going well. He is worthy of our adoration every second of every day—no matter the situation. Living this out takes a good dose of faith.

Father, it isn't easy to put on a garment of praise every day. There are sometimes I just don't feel like smiling or being happy. I thank you that I can choose to have a good attitude in those moments. I can choose to be thankful simply because you have given me another day to live.

God Hears My Prayers

In the same way the Spirit also helps our
weakness; for we do not know how to
pray as we should, but the Spirit Himself
intercedes for us with groanings too
deep for words; and He who searches the
hearts knows what the mind of the Spirit
is, because He intercedes for the saints
according to the will of God.

Romans 8:26-27 NASB

It is an amazing and powerful thing that the Holy Spirit
within us can recognize the Holy Spirit in another believer.
It unites people across geographic, economic, generational,
and cultural boundaries. Two souls, surrendered to the same
Savior, have plenty in common.

This miraculous connection can also bring us closer to God
when we allow the Holy Spirit to show us how. When we are

too weak in our flesh to know how or what to pray, we can count on the Holy Spirit to show us the way. What a relief!

When the words don't seem to come out right or our supplications feel empty, we can submit to the Holy Spirit to intercede for us with prayers beyond mere words. God hears his children. And he hears his Spirit in a language that only the holy can utter.

Believe that God hears your prayers. And just as two women with only Jesus in common can bond over their Messiah, the Holy Spirit in you will never run out of things to mediate to the Father. Cry out, however you can, and know that he hears every word.

Father, I thank you that you are always listening and that you care about me. I pour out my heart to you and ask you for wisdom and grace to walk through each day.

Look to the Lord and his strength; seek his face always.

1 CHRONICLES 16:11 NIV

Protected

You have been a defense for the helpless,
a defense for the needy in his distress,
a refuge from the storm, a shade from the heat.

Isaiah 25:4 NASB

In Christ, we are protected. We have a strong shield, a faithful defender, and a constant guardian. Many have mistaken this promise as a guarantee against pain, suffering, or hardship. When sorrows overwhelm us, can we stay faithful to our protector? Will we interpret adversity as betrayal, or embrace a protection that sometimes involves endurance, anguish, and pain?

Protection does not mean perfection. Can we trust God only when our lives follow a path of ease? Faith gives depth to our expectations; we may not see through the dark clouds of the storm, but we know that God has prepared us for them.

No matter how hard the rain falls or how fast the winds blow, we believe in his protection over us as we pass through the storm. God's security shelters us according to what we need, not necessarily from what pains us.

The storms will rage and the heat will blister, each in their turn and maybe for a long time. Can you believe that he is protecting you through it all? His hand is upon you, defending and sheltering you. Let no storm shake your faith in this.

God, I see your hand of protection over my life, even when things aren't going as I hope. Thank you for deepening my faith as I recognize that you are with me in all of my storms. You don't leave me and you won't let me drown.

Provision

"Ask and it will be given to you; seek and
you will find; knock and the door will be
opened to you. For everyone who asks
receives; the one who seeks finds; and to the
one who knocks, the door
will be opened."

Matthew 7:7-8 NIV

Because of God's great and perfect knowledge, you can trust
that he understands you, from your deepest depths to your
highest heights. He knows what lies behind you and he can
heal your wounds. He knows what lies ahead of you, and he
can prepare you for victory.

In Christ, we are given everything we need to shoulder our
burdens; we are humble enough to suffer and patient enough
to persevere. He strengthens us in our season of need,
not before, and sometimes the strength fades so quickly
afterward that we wonder how the feat was accomplished.

God asks us to press into him because much prayer is needed for the seasons to come. Gather the oil of faith now, for the days are coming when we will pour out from what we have stored up. He waits patiently for us to cry out for help.

God's provisions are personal to each believer. Only you can receive what he offers because you are the one knocking at his door! When he opens it, ask him all those questions you've been wanting answers to. How should I worship? What does devotion look like? How do you want me to overcome sin? You will receive everything you need when you trust the great provider.

*God, I am knocking on your door again
asking you to provide for me.
I know you care about my needs,
and I know you want to answer my
deepest questions. Speak clearly to me
today as I draw near to you.*

Specific Purpose

We are God's handiwork, created in Christ
Jesus to do good works, which God
prepared in advance for us to do.

Ephesians 2:10 NIV

Very few people know exactly what they want to be *when they grow up*. We take multiple tests to find out our personality types, strengths, and spiritual gifts, all to determine what we should do with our lives.

While these tests can be good indicators of suitable opportunities, the best way to find the perfect fit is to go directly to the source.

No matter what you may have been told, you were planned by God. That means he put you on this earth for a very specific reason. God's desire is that you will partner with him in that plan. When you begin to walk in his purpose, you will find the joy, peace, strength, and grace you need to carry it out.

Choose to believe that God has a purpose for your life, and start asking him to reveal it to you. Don't place limitations on him. He can do great things through you if you are willing to trust him.

God, you know what I love to do. You know what makes me excited about the day. Thank you for placing desires in me that suit me. I believe you have something special for me to do. And I believe it falls in line with what you have made me passionate about because that is just what you are like!

God Sees Everything

Let us not grow weary of doing good, for in
due season we will reap, if we do not give up.

Galatians 6:9 ESV

"Look at me! Look at me! Watch this!" Oh how often children
seek recognition from just about anyone who will watch.
Even though the dive bomb into the water looks exactly
the same as it did last time, or the cartwheel is still lopsided
after thirty attempts, onlookers continue to encourage the
repetitious behavior.

Are we really very different from those children? Don't we
also look for recognition in life? "Look at me; I made dinner
every night this week!" "See this awesome presentation I put
together for work?" "You should have seen the smiles on the
faces of those people I helped today." We want someone to
notice our efforts, our charity, our diligence, our excellence.
And, though we hate to admit it, we may even get a little
upset if nobody does.

We can choose to search for recognition from others, or we can believe that God sees everything we do. Because he does. He is interested in that project we worked so hard on. He is delighted when we spend our time serving others. He loves it when we do our very best.

Don't waste your time trying to be recognized by others. Share your talents and abilities *without holding back!* Your Father in heaven has his eye on you, and he's not about to look away.

God, I am so grateful that you recognize me. You are watching and applauding and encouraging me. Help me when I feel like giving up to remember that I will reap a harvest of blessing if I continue doing good. You are watching, and that's all that matters.

God
is our refuge
and strength,
a very
present help
in trouble.

PSALM 46:1 ESV

I Am Redeemed

"Truly, truly, I say to you, whoever hears my word and believes him who sent me has eternal life. He does not come into judgment, but has passed from death to life. Truly, truly, I say to you, an hour is coming, and is now here, when the dead will hear the voice of the Son of God, and those who hear will live."

John 5:24-25 ESV

Because of Jesus Christ, we get to start over. His grace covers us and we receive his mercies anew each morning. Because of Jesus Christ, we dipped into everlasting pools of healing, baptized by the cool and refreshing presence of the Holy Spirit. We approached the throne humble, expectant, and thirsty because we could no longer shoulder the weight of our sins.

Burdens unloaded at the foot of the throne; we were redeemed for freedom and live now in the promise of life everlasting. We have *passed from death to life.* We have the assurance of our redemption, but do we live like the redeemed every day? Do we rejoice like slaves who have been set free?

Redeemed, we abandon the path once walked for the one navigated by God. Slaves cannot determine their steps; they are ordered to walk. But children of God have been ransomed and set free. They must choose to run from the paths of materialism, pride, vanity, and idolatry that have been paved by the world.

Being redeemed means being reinvented, refurbished, and revitalized. Something broken, ugly, or useless is given purpose. We are given a purpose in our redemption: to show those still in bondage how to break free from their chains.

Thank you, God, for the redemptive work of your Son in my life. You have erased every sin I have confessed, and I am eternally grateful.

Rest in God

Bless the LORD, O my soul,
and forget not all his benefits,
who forgives all your iniquity,
who heals all your diseases,
who redeems your life from the pit,
who crowns you with steadfast love and mercy,
who satisfies you with good
so that your youth is renewed
like the eagle's.

Psalm 103:2-5 ESV

Is it reasonable to believe that a marathon runner can finish a race without a single refreshing cup of water? Would it be fair to expect a doctor, after working a 36-hour shift, to have the energy to perform one last tedious surgery? Can a child be expected not to lick the spatula that mixed the cookie dough? Or should a foreigner be intuitively familiar with the customs of a new land?

We know that humans have limits. We need to eat and drink regularly. We get tired and struggle if we don't have enough sleep. We learn patience and self-control as we get older, but our emotions can be overwhelmed by life's great upheavals.

The shepherd king, David, knew this and understood God's gracious and loving path of refreshment.

Whether you are at peak performance or running on empty, needing renewal now or in the future, God alone can give you what you need for the refreshment of your mind, body, and spirit because he knows your limits and capabilities. He knows that you need time to refuel, space to recover your strength, and that sometimes a little cookie dough goes a long way.

Rest in God when you need to be refreshed. Don't believe that you aren't strong because you need to rest; you aren't meant be strong forever. You are designed to lean on the one whose strength can renew you.

God, I need your strength to renew me. Thank you that you want me to ask you for rest and refreshment every time I need it. Help me to remember to come to you for peace instead of seeking it out in other places.

Not Disappointed

Those who love me, I will deliver;
I will protect those who know my name.
When they call to me, I will answer them;
I will be with them in trouble,
I will rescue them and honor them.

Psalm 91:14-15 NRSV

There's something to be said for a reliable car. It starts *every* time you turn the key over. It *never* breaks down and leaves you stranded in the middle of a highway. It *always* blows heat in the cold of winter and cold air in the heat of summer.

If we want our cars to be reliable, we want people to be even more so. They *always* show up when they say they will. They *never* forget to finish their part of an important project. *Every* time you call, they pick up the phone.

We know that neither cars nor people are completely reliable. What we do know is that both cars and people will fail us at some point in our lives. It's inevitable. Aren't you glad to be in relationship with someone who cannot fail you because it is not in his nature to fail—*ever*?

Our perfect God is always near. He doesn't forget about our important plans or our hopes and dreams. He won't be caught off guard when it's our birthday, anniversary, graduation day, important final interview, or anything in between.

> *God, you want what is best for me and*
> *you have the means to see it happen.*
> *Help me to keep my focus on you so*
> *that I will not be disappointed. You will*
> *never fail me.*

"My grace is all you need. My power works best in weakness."

2 CORINTHIANS
12:9 NLT

The Only Opinion

O LORD my God,
you have performed many wonders for us.
Your plans for us are too numerous to list.
You have no equal.
If I tried to recite all your wonderful deeds,
I would never come to the end of them.
"I take joy in doing your will, my God,
for your instructions are written on my heart."

Psalm 40:5, 8 NLT

God created you for relationship with him, just as he created Adam and Eve. He delights in your voice, your laughter, and your ideas. He longs to fellowship with you just as he did with his first son and daughter. But, like Adam and Eve, we are sometimes persuaded by the opinions of others instead of listening and obeying the commands of our Father and greatest friend.

It is understandably tempting to share our grievances, triumphs, problems, or desires with friends and loved ones we can easily call on the phone or meet for coffee. God has given us wonderful relationships! But we run the risk of listening first to their opinions rather than God's, and this risk can trap us in sin.

When life gets difficult, we can run to him with our frustrations. When we're overwhelmed with sadness or grief, we can carry our pain to him. In the heat of anger or frustration, we can call on him for freedom. He is a friend that offers all of this—and more—in mercy and love, and he is worthy of our friendship.

Don't let others' opinions of you matter more than God's. Train your heart to run first to God with your pain, joy, frustration, and excitement. His friendship will never let you down!

Father, it's hard to believe that you want to share in my everyday moments. I want to value your opinion above all others and be content in just knowing that you delight in me.

Lifted Up

You, O Lord, are a shield about me,
My glory, and the One who lifts my head.

Psalm 3:3 NASB

Picture a young girl running a race. She leaps off to a great start when the gun sounds. She pushes her way to the front of the pack in no time and sets a pace that is tough to compete with. As she rounds the final corner with the finish line in sight, she stumbles. She tries desperately to regain her balance, but it's too late. She crashes to the ground.

Trying to be brave, she jumps up and sprints the final yards to complete the race. Fourth place.

Head hung low, skinned knees burning, and vision blurry, she walks over to her coach. He gently lifts her chin to the sun, and brushes away the tears that have spilled over.

As her bottom lip begins to quiver, he reassures her that everything is going to be okay. That life is full of painful moments that creep up unexpectedly, but it's also full of second chances. "Don't give up on yourself," he says, "I haven't given up on you."

When we've given up, run away, lost the plot, or stumbled and fallen, God doesn't give up on us. When we come to him with our heads hung low, he lifts our chins, looks intently into our eyes, and whispers tender words of compassion that reach the deepest places in our hearts.

> *Father, sometimes I don't feel like I can look up. I need your comforting words to wash over my wounds and bring healing to my heart. Tip my chin to the sky and tell me that you love me, God. I need to hear that from you so desperately.*

Truly Understood

Jesus… understands our weaknesses, for
he faced all of the same testings we do, yet
he did not sin. So let us come boldly to the
throne of our gracious God. There we will
receive his mercy, and we will find grace to
help us when we need it most.

Hebrews 4:15-16 NLT

Don't lose heart. Guard your faith and listen to God's voice.
He understands your love for him. You may think it's small or
diminishing, but he knows it is strong and full. You love like a
child—believing and carefree.

Keep your eyes fixed on God. He understands your needs.
He is your refuge and strength. Only he can sustain you.
He is your stream of water, your living sacrifice, your good
shepherd. He is your comfort and his mercy is complete.

God understands your heart and all its pains, sorrows, longings, and disappointments, and he comforts you. He will never leave you or forsake you. He loves you too much.

Whatever you need, you can ask God and he will answer you; he already knows what you long for. Nothing is a surprise to him. Know that he truly understands your heart. He knows the test you are facing, and he gives you the mercy you need to endure it. *When you need it most,* his grace is there.

> *Thank you, God, for your deep understanding of my heart. You know me so well, and you care about all the details of my life. You are not put off by my weaknesses or faults. You see them and you love me anyway because you truly know me.*

I prayed
to the Lord,
and he
answered me.
He freed me
from all my
fears.

PSALM 34:4 NLT

Wisdom in Every Situation

Then you will understand
what is right, just, and fair,
and you will find the right way to go.
For wisdom will enter your heart,
and knowledge will fill you with joy.
Wise choices will watch over you.
Understanding will keep you safe.

Proverbs 2:9-11 NLT

All of life is a test. As we live each day, the tests we face teach us valuable lessons. It may seem backwards: usually lessons are learned to prepare us for a test. But in life, the test often comes first. Through the lessons, God gives us the wisdom we need for the next test.

It's a safe bet that the tests will keep coming. Thankfully, our hearts gain understanding every time. Tension and uncertainty melt away; joy blossoms.

Solomon's advice is that we listen to wisdom, apply it, and learn as we go. Then we will have understanding; we will find the right path with wisdom in our hearts and joy from knowledge. We will be safe. *Yes, please.*

Gaining wisdom doesn't guarantee that you won't stumble and fall on your face or stick your foot in your mouth. You will still make mistakes, say the wrong thing at the wrong time, and wish you could go back in time and do it right. It stings.

Even when we fail the test, we learn a lesson and gain wisdom... if we humble ourselves. We can trust that God will give us wisdom in every situation. Another test is just around the corner, waiting for us to pass with flying colors!

> *God, I have learned so many valuable lessons from life's tests! I take joy in the wisdom I have gained from those tests. Thank you for giving me the opportunity to make wise choices.*

The Truth of God's Word

Your words are true from the start,
and all your laws will be fair forever.
I am as happy over your promises
as if I had found a great treasure.

Psalm 119:160, 162 NCV

The world shouts, "Truth is relative!" "Truth is what I believe!" "Truth is what I want it to be!" We cannot entertain these lies. Truth is found in God's Word alone.

Truth is absolute. It has not changed since the beginning of time and it will not change on into eternity.

Because God's Word is true, we can believe everything it says. It's by far not the most popular thing to stake our morals, beliefs, and decisions on, and we can be sure to expect a good amount of opposition and ridicule when we do.

It's important to surround ourselves with others who also believe wholeheartedly in the absolute nature of God's Word. Stand together in faith and declare that God's Word is the definition of truth itself.

Knowing the truth and believing it means that we get to believe in all of the promises in God's Word. His promises are good and true. They are promises that show us how deeply he loves and cares for us. They are promises of justice, mercy, and kindness. This should make us, as the Psalmist says, as happy as if we have found great treasure—because we actually have!

God, I choose to stand on the truth of your Word in this season of my life. Whether that is easy or difficult doesn't matter. I believe in the absolute truth of your promises, and this alone brings me joy.

You will
seek me
and find me
when you
seek me
with all
your heart.

JEREMIAH 29:13 NIV